I Miss You Today

Maureen Nelson

BookLocker

Trenton, Georgia

Paperback ISBN: 978-1-958877-81-4
Hardcover ISBN: 978-1-958877-82-1

Published by BookLocker.com, Inc., Trenton, Georgia, U.S.A.

Printed on acid-free paper.

BookLocker.com, Inc.
2022

Inspirations:

My grandson, Riggins, who taught me what is most important — compassion, courage, love, and laughter. My daughter Ashley and son-in-law Josh, for their unwavering faith, strength, and commitment to giving Riggins an extraordinary life. My daughter, Sarah, my son-in-law Josh, my son, Jesse, and my daughter-in-law Sarah, for their support, encouragement, and love. All my grandchildren, for the pure joy they bring. My husband, Dave, for always being there for me. I am so grateful to do life with him by my side.
I love you all!

Acknowledgements:

A special thank you to Heather Siegel for agreeing, without hesitation, to bring this book to life with her amazing and beautiful talent.

To see more of Heather's art, visit dragonflyconnectionarts.com

To Kevin J Ward, for encouraging me to write, for his wisdom through the process and for his lifelong friendship.

To Steve Guider, for helping me put the final details together.

And now these three remain: faith, hope and love. But the greatest of these is love.

1 Corinthians 13:13

I miss you today, I'll miss you tomorrow.

I miss waking in the morning to see your

bristly, bushy, bedhead hair.

I miss cuddling with you on the big brown chair while

Mommy reads us a story.

I miss helping you learn how to gently turn the pages.

I miss watching you wave and wiggle with glee as the school bus rounds the corner.

I miss hearing your giddy giggles as I ran behind pushing you faster and faster.

I miss riding in the car while you would slyly sneak to snatch my hat.

I miss listening to your big belly laugh as Daddy swung you way up high.

I miss you today, I'll miss you tomorrow.

So, when I have an ache in my tummy and feel bad, I'll remember all the joy you still had.

When I put my glasses on my nose, I'll remember your grin before you flung yours down to your toes.

When I sit on the porch and look up at the stars, I'll
know the brightest one is yours.

When I'm feeling scared and afraid, I'll remember how
you were so brave.

When I'm cranky and it's hard to be kind, I'll remember your smile from ear to ear when a new friend you would find.

When It's time for bed and I start to pray, I'll thank Jesus for you and this beautiful day.

I miss you today, I'll miss you tomorrow.

"Riggins"

Riggins entered the world on February 20, 2011, about seven weeks ahead of his due date. Despite his early arrival, he was a healthy boy. As he was our first child, we didn't see anything other than perfection when we brought him home. Six months later, doctors noticed he wasn't hitting some of the typical milestones and we started searching for answers. Within a few weeks, Riggins was diagnosed with Congenital Disorder of Glycosylation Type 1A (CDG). CDG is a rare genetic disorder that causes global developmental delay along with a host of other health issues. The type and severity of health problems vary greatly for each person with CDG which makes this rare disorder more difficult to navigate. For myself, learning of Riggins diagnosis was a process and I needed to grieve the loss of the boy I thought we would have, and instead look forward and celebrate the boy he was and would become. Being with Riggins made that process easier as his sweet personality and infectious laugh began to show more and more. Riggins always loved being on the move, whether that was a car ride, a walk, or getting pushed in his wheelchair on a wild ride from his younger brothers. He participated in Miracle League baseball and football camp, but Riggins really loved any opportunity to be with kids. Riggins never used words to communicate, but it was easy to tell what he wanted. He leaned into you while lying on the couch and put his hand on yours when he wanted to be close. His desire was to be with you, and he made you feel special when he was. Riggins captured people with his gentle spirit and his genuine enthusiasm. Riggins was a light to all, and he always saved a smile for everyone he met. Even in his last moments on earth, his light was bright, and he was always just as perfect as that day we brought him home from the hospital. Riggins passed away peacefully at home on November 15, 2019.

Forever Riggins Dad,

Josh

CPSIA information can be obtained
at www.ICGtesting.com
Printed in the USA
BVHW091427171222
654335BV00008B/504

9 781958 877814